First edition 1996

ISBN 7 – 5052 – 0316 – 9

Published by China Esperanto Press, Beijing
24 Baiwanzhuang Road, Beijing,
China, 100037
P. O. Box 399, Post code: 100044
Distributed by China International Book Trading Corporation (Guoji Shudian)
35 Chegongzhuang Xilu, Beijing, China
05000

# 北京长城

# The Great wall in Beijing

China Esperanto Press, Beijing

中国世界语出版社 北京

# 长城泛议

万里长城是世界上最著名、最宏伟、最壮观的古代奇迹之一。它像一条巨龙，从鸭绿江畔起身，翻越巍巍群山，穿过茫茫草原，跨越浩瀚沙漠，奔向世界屋脊帕米尔高原。万里长城望不断的城楼雉堞、雄关隘口、亭障墩堠，把中国北方点缀得绚丽多彩。

长城的修建，绵延持续了两千多年。开始于公元前 7 世纪前后，当时，中国正处于诸侯纷争的春秋时期，各诸侯国为了互相防御，纷纷在自己的领土上修筑了高大的城墙。由于这种城墙很长，而且不是周圈封闭的，所以称作长城或长垣。

中国历史上修筑长城工程最浩大的有三朝。

一是秦朝(公元前 221～前 206 年)为保障国家统一，抵御北方匈奴侵扰而修筑的长城。秦长城西起临洮(今甘肃岷县)，东至辽东，长达一万多华里，是中国第一条万里长城。

汉代(公元前 206～公元 220 年)大规模修筑长城，将秦长城延伸到新疆罗布泊以西，长达两万多华里。

明朝(公元 1368～1644 年)是修筑长城的最后一个朝代。明长城东起鸭绿江畔，西至嘉峪关，全长一万三千多华里。明长城设计讲究，工程浩大，防御功能完备。

据历史记载，有二十多个诸侯国和王朝修筑过长城，总长 10 万 8 千华里。如果将其变成厚 1 米、高 5 米的土石厚墙，可环绕地球十几周。

如此规模宏大而又艰巨的工程，在劳动力调配、材料来源、规划设计和施工等方面都是相当庞大复杂的。古代的中国人是怎样解决这些问题的呢？

修筑长城的人力，主要是军队。如秦始皇时修筑长城，即是大将军蒙恬在打退匈奴后，以 30 万大军修筑的。强迫征调的民夫是修长城的重要力量。秦始皇时除了几十万军队外,还强征了大约五十万民夫。再就是发配充军的犯人。秦汉时,有一种刑罚叫"城旦",就是将犯人剃成光头,颈上加上铁圈,送去修筑长城。

修建长城的材料,在没有大量用砖以前,主要是土、石、木料、瓦件等,一般为就地取材。在高山峻岭,则在山上开取石料,用石块砌筑;在平原黄土地带便就地取土夯筑;在沙漠地区还采用了芦苇或红柳枝条层层铺沙的办法,如新疆罗布泊一带的汉长城就是这样修筑的。在东北还有用柞木编制的木栅墙,用木板做的木板墙。

修筑长城的施工十分艰巨。旧时的长城沿线,不是高山深谷,就是沙漠草原,又没有先进的施工机具和运输工具,施工之难可想而知。如我们今天在居庸关、八达岭所见到的长城,砌墙用的条石有的长达3米,重两千多斤。而长城随着险峻的山脊修筑,坡度十分陡峭,游人徒手上城还感到吃力,当时修筑的人们要把两千多斤的大条石、数十斤重的大城砖和大量的石灰运上山去,其困难可想而知。

根据记载和传说,搬运方法有几种。

主要是人力搬运。用人背、肩扛、筐挑、杠子抬、传递等办法将大量的城砖、石块搬运上去,这是最原始最吃力的办法。除此之外,还利用简单的机具,如手推小车,这是用在比较平缓的山坡上;在运送上千斤的大石上山时则采用滚木和撬棍,并且在山上安置绞盘将巨大石块绞上去;在跨过深沟狭谷运送砖瓦和石灰时,采用了"飞筐走索"的办法,即把砖瓦石灰装在筐内从两岸拉固的绳索上滑溜过去,大大节省了劳力。

因为大量的运输和修筑工作都靠笨重的人力来完成,所以进展缓慢。八达岭长城上发现一块明朝修筑长城的石碑,记载着万历十年(公元1582年)用了几千名官兵加上许多民夫,才包修了七十多丈(约合200米)的一段长城，可见工程的艰巨了。

正如石碑所反映的，长城的修筑主要是与防守任务相统一，采用分区、分片、分段包干的办法。如汉朝河西四郡(武威、张掖、酒泉、敦煌)的长城就是由四郡的郡守负责各自境内长城的修筑，郡再把任务分摊到各段、各防守据点的戍卒身上去。当然大工程和关城则要由郡守调集力量去修筑。中央政权也从全国各地征调军队和募集劳力到重点地区去修筑。

花费众多人力，费尽千辛万苦修筑的长城，当时是作为防御工事存在的。如果以现代战争的眼光来看，城墙自然起不到多大作用。但是，在以刀枪、弓箭、戈矛等为武器作战的古代，情况就完全不同了。城坚墙高，据城固守，确实能起到非常重要的作用。特别是对付那些飘忽不定的游动骑兵，这种坚固的防御工事是非常必要的。中国历史上几次大规模修筑长城，都是受北边游牧民族威胁最厉害的时候，如秦汉受匈奴、明受蒙古族的威胁。

经过两千多年的不断修筑和完善，万里长城形成了一个从中央政权通过各级军事、行政机构，联系最基层军事单位及守城戍卒的完整防御体系。以明朝为例，长城沿线分设辽东、蓟、宣府、大同等九个镇。每镇设总兵，指挥本镇所辖长城沿线的兵马，平时守卫本镇长城，有警时受兵部或皇帝特派大臣的指挥，救援其他镇的防务。每镇兵员约十万左右，随长城防守的需要时有增减。如明隆庆年间(公元 1567~1572 年)宣府镇额兵151452 名，大同镇额兵 135778 名。九镇兵员共在一百万人上下。每镇之下又按不同情况分为许多"路"。每个"路"包括许多"关"以及城堡、墩台等等。例如，山海路包括山海关、南海口关等关口。关口、城堡之下又管辖一些城楼、敌台和烽火台。巡防的戍卒用呼喊传递或烽火为号，经由各级军事组织,将敌情一直传报到朝廷。

戍守长城的百万士卒,最初是轮流看守,一年或几年换班。这样频繁调动,劳民伤财,于国于民都不利。后来,在相对太平时期,除一些险关重隘仍由军队把守外,其他地方皆由"楼军"看管。所谓"楼军",实际是由内地迁到长城的百姓,他们被实行军事管制,偕妻带子,住在敌楼里,一旦发现敌情,赶紧点火报警。这在明代中期已成惯例。

"楼军"一家人的生活全部自给。他们每一家在山沟低洼处打眼小井,供一家人使用。按照朝廷规定,"楼军"一年只能刨 365 个埯种庄稼,每天吃一个埯里打出的粮食。如果谁省吃俭用剩下了粮食,得统统交公。"楼军"世代相传,有的人家几辈子住在敌楼里,不知道住普通房子是啥滋味。

上下两千年,纵横十万余里的长城,是中国历史上各民族间金戈铁马、逐鹿争雄的见证。然而,随着时代的发展,国家的统一,中华民族的大团结,它早已完成了历史使命,昔日的战场变成了名胜古迹。北京地区的长城因其险峻雄伟尤受中外游人的青睐。

明代建都北京,为捍卫京师和皇帝祖陵,十分注重北京地区长城的修建。所以北京长城是明长城中工程最浩大、建筑最坚固、设计最精美、防御设施最完备、保存最完整的一段,是古长城之精华。窥一斑而见全豹。游人参观北京地段的长城可以了解整个古长城的全貌。因此,本画册集中篇幅介绍了北京长城的四大景点,同时还介绍了万里长城的起点和终点。北京长城全长 629 公里,有城台 827 座,关口 71 座,现已开发的旅游点有八达岭、慕田峪、金山岭、司马台等处。这些地方已成为文化交流、旅游观光、激发热情、锻炼意志、健美减肥的极佳胜地,中外游人络绎不绝。

# About the Great Wall

The Great Wall is one of the ancient construction wonders in the world. It traverses immense deserts, high mountains and broad grasslands in the northern part of China from east to west. The many watch towers, beacon towers, passes and garrison castles add more magnificence to the Great Wall.

Construction of the Great Wall began in the 7th century B.C. Warlords were fighting for hegemony. They built long walls along their borders to defend their domain. In 221 B.C. Qin Shihuang defeated all the warlords, unified China, gave himself the title First Emperor. He ordered to link up some of these long walls to ward off raids of the Huns to the north. The project went on until the end of the Qin Dynasty in 206 B.C. The Qin Great Wall began in Lintao (present-day Minxian County in Gansu Province) in the west and ended in Liaodong Peninsula in the east, over 5,000 kilometers long.

A large-scale project on the Great Wall was carried out during the Han Dynasty (206 B.C.-A.D. 220). The Great Wall was extended toward the west for another 5,000 kilometers to Lop Nur Lake in today's Xinjiang Uygur Autonomous Region.

The last large-scale project on the Great Wall was carried out in the Ming Dynasty (1368-1644). The Ming Great Wall was 6,500 kilometers long from the Yalu River in the east to Jiayuguan Pass in the west. This ancient defense work became perfect.

History records show that over 2,000 years two dozen dukedoms and dynasties built defense walls of a total length of 54,000 kilometers. If they were put together as a wall one meter thick and five meters high, it would go around the earth more than 10 times. Such gigantic work required complicated management of manpower, materials and planning. How could the Chinese in ancient times with primitive tools have accomplished this?

The main force for the work was composed of soldiers defending the frontier. Emperor Qin Shihuang sent his army commander Meng Tian and

300,000 troops to guard against the Huns in the north. The army was also assigned to link up various defense walls built by warlords. Another work force comprised exiles. During the Qin Dynasty half a million exiles were sent to build the Great Wall. Their heads were shaved and an iron ring was put around their necks to mark their status. A great number of conscripts were also used.

In the beginning the building materials were earth, stone, wood and pottery tiles. In mountain areas, stone was quarried; on the plains the wall was built with rammed clay; in the deserts, the wall was built with reeds and willow branch nets to hold sands. The part near Lop Nur Lake was built this way. In Northeast China some sections of the Great Wall were piles of oak timber.

The Great Wall runs mostly in mountains and deserts. Without machinery the job was difficult. Stone blocks with which the sections of the Great Wall at Juyongguan Pass and Badaling Hill were built are three meters long and weigh more than 1,000 kilograms a piece. Some parts of the mountainsides are very steep. Today people feel difficult to climb the up them without carrying anything. But the construction workers had to move the heavy stone blocks and other materials with their bare hands.

The common transportation method was to carry building materials on people's bare backs and shoulders, with baskets or poles. Simple means such as wheelbarrows could be used on flat land or gentle mountain slopes. Raw wood poles and crowbars were used to roll large stone blocks up a mountain. More ingenious ways included cables over deep gullies or rivers to convey baskets filled with lime, bricks or tiles.

Since most of the work was done manually, construction was very slow. A stone inscription unearthed at Badaling records that in 1582 during the Ming Dynasty a section of 200 meters took several thousand soldiers and conscripts to finish in a whole year.

The construction and repair of the Great Wall was closely related to defense. The work was divided into a number of sections and each garrison commander was responsible for the completion of the section within his territory. For incidence, the imperial court of the Han Dynasty assigned the construction work to the governors of four prefectures (Wuwei, Zhangye, Jiuquan and Dunhuang), each responsible for a part of The Great Wall. The governors in turn allocated the task to their officers who were also responsible for the defense of the area where the section of the Great Wall was to be built. The governors would send more troops for major projects at key points. The central government helped by sending conscripts to the construction sites.

The Great Wall had lost its significance of defense in modern times. But in ancient times when main weapons were spears, swords and arrows the Great Wall played a very important strategic role. It had guarded against the constant raids of nomadic horsemen to the north of it. All the several large-scale construction and repair projects were carried out in Chinese history only when there were invasions of nomadic tribes from the north—Huns in the Qin and Han dynasties and Mongols in the Ming Dynasty.

In 2,000 years the Great Wall became a complete defense work with close-knit administrative layers from the imperial court down to the defense soldiers. For example, during the Ming Dynasty, the imperial court set up nine commands along the Great Wall, including Liaodong, Ji, Xuanfu and Datong. The commandant was in charge of the troops defending the section of the Great Wall. During a war the commandants were under the direct leadership of the Ministry of Defense or an envoy of the emperor. They also had the responsibility to aid each other. The number of troops for each command was about 100,000. More troops would be sent when a war was impending. During the Longqing Period (1567-1572) of the Ming Dynasty, the Xuanfu Command had 15,1452 troops and the Datong Command had 135,778 troops. The total number of soldiers of the nine commands came to one million.

Each command was further divided into several "routes" which were in charge of a number of defense castles, passes and watch towers. For incidence, the Shanhai Route had Shanhai Pass and Nanhai Pass to protect. The passes and defense castles were in turn responsible for a number of watch towers and beacon towers. Patrol soldiers passed information either by words or fire signals. Such information was passed on to the court through various military units.

In the beginning one million soldiers of the Great Wall worked on shifts of one year or several years. Such shifting was too costly. So the court decided to put the regular army at key points while let other parts of the Great Wall be watched by "tower soldiers". The tower soldiers were actually civilians under military regimental control. They and their families lived in the watch towers and would send fire signals when there was danger of raids of nomadic tribes. Such practice became established in the middle of the Ming Dynasty.

The tower soldiers had to support their families by growing food themselves. The court allowed each family to reclaim 365 spots of land and eat the harvest of one spot in one day. The food saved at the end of the year must be turned to their superiors. The tower soldiers' job was inheritable. They lived in the watch towers all their lives.

After the Ming Dynasty set up its capital in Beijing, the imperial court paid great attention to the preservation of the Great Wall near it. It spent great amounts of funds and manpower on its repair. The sections of the Ming Great Wall near Beijing are the best and strongest. The Great Wall, which had seen numerous battles, has become a historic site for tourists. The sections near Beijing are more attractive for their well-preserved conditions and their nearness to the national capital.

This picture album describes the Great Wall near Beijing at Badaling, Mutianyu, Jinshanling and Simatai over 629 kilometers with 827 watch towers and 71 passes.

# 居庸关和八达岭

北京西北 50 余公里处,有一条长 18.5 公里的峡谷,叫"关沟"。这里是北京西北的门户,从南到北设有四重关口:南口、居庸关、上关、八达岭。峡谷两旁层峦叠嶂,草木葱茏,景色非常优美,自古誉为"居庸叠翠",是燕京八景之一。

居庸关是万里长城最负盛名的雄关之一。两侧高山耸峙,峭壁陡不可攀,关城雄踞其中,扼控着南下北京的通道。这种绝险的地势,决定了它在军事上的重要性。这里曾导演出几场决定朝廷命运的战争。北宋宣和四年(公元 1122 年)金(公元 1115～1234 年)灭辽(公元 907～1125 年),就是攻取居庸关后挥师南进,直取辽都燕京(即今北京)。明军灭元(公元 1206～1368 年),也是先攻下居庸关,而后长驱直入,一举攻占元大都北京城。277 年后,李自成农民起义军,又是攻取居庸关,而后进北京,推翻了腐朽的明王朝。

八达岭是居庸关的重要前哨,北往延庆,西去宣化、张家口、大同,东至唐山、承德。交通四通八达,故名八达岭。它是明代首都北京的重要屏障,居高临下,地势险峻。它要路雄踞,可说是"一夫当关,万夫莫开",比居庸关更险要。所以古人说,"居庸之险不在关而在八达岭"。


# Juyongguan Pass and the Great Wall at Badaling

A 18.5-kilometer-long valley lies 50 kilometers northwest of downtown Beijing. The mountains flanking the valley have many graceful peaks and luxuriant trees and plants. Along it from north to south are four passes on the Great Wall: Nankou, Juyongguan, Shangguan and Badaling. They used to be of great strategic importance in defending the national capital Beijing.

Juyongguan Pass, one of the most famous passes of the Great Wall, is located above a gap between mountain peaks. A road leading to the capital from the north passes through it. In history it witnessed several battles that decided the fate of the country. In 1122 the army of the Jin regime (1115-1234) took the Juyongguan Pass and went on to Beijing to overthrow the Liao Dynasty (907-1125). The troops of the Ming Dynasty first took the pass before they took Beijing, capital of the Yuan Dynasty (1206-1368). A peasants' uprising army led by Li Zicheng did the same in 1644 to overthrow the Ming Dynasty.

Badaling Pass was an outpost of Juyongguan Pass. "Bada" in Chinese means convenient transportation. Roads beginning from Badaling lead to Yanqing, Xuanhua, Zhangjiakou, Datong, Yongning and Sihai. Rising high on a mountain ridge it used to be more important than Juyongguan in the defense of Beijing during the Ming Dynasty. A saying described Badaling Pass: "It needs only one man to block the advance of ten thousand troops."

**远眺居庸关城** 雄关两侧青山夹峙,长城围合,
地势险要,素为兵家必争之地。

**An aerial view of Juyongguan Pass** The Great
Wall stretches toward either side from Juyongguan
Pass. In ancient times it was of vital importance
in the defense of Beijing.

**居庸关全景** 居庸之名,缘起于"徙居庸徒"(庸是贫苦受雇的劳力)。据说秦始皇修筑长城时,将强征来的民夫士卒迁居于此。其城垣创建于明景泰(公元 1450～1456 年)初。

**Juyongguan Pass** Juyong in Chinese means "a place of poor laborers". Emperor Qin Shihuang forced many conscripts to build this part of the Great Wall. The present wall was rebuilt between 1450 and 1456 during the Ming Dynasty.

**金翅鸟**　云台券门正中刻有金翅鸟王,两旁刻有交叉金刚杆图案和大象、猛龙、卷叶花和大蟒神,雕刻精美,栩栩如生。

**'Golden-Winged Bird'**　In the middle of the arched passage of the Cloud Terrace is a carving of 'Golden-Winged Bird' flanked by carved designs of elephants, dragons, snakes and plants with curved leaves.

**云台**　位于居庸关城内,建于元至正五年(公元1345年),台上曾先后建过喇嘛塔和泰安佛寺,下面是北京到蒙古的大路,故又名"过街塔"。台用汉白玉砌成,高9.5米,下基东西长26.8米,南北长17.6米,其上雕刻着精美的浮雕,有很高的艺术价值。

**Yuntai (Cloud Terrace)**　The marble terrace was built in 1345 inside Juyongguan Pass. There used to be a lamaist pagoda and Tai'an Temple on it. A road passes under it from north to south. The terrace is 9.5 meters high, 26.8 meters from east to west and 17.6 meters from north to south at the base. The carvings in relief on the terrace are of high artistic level.

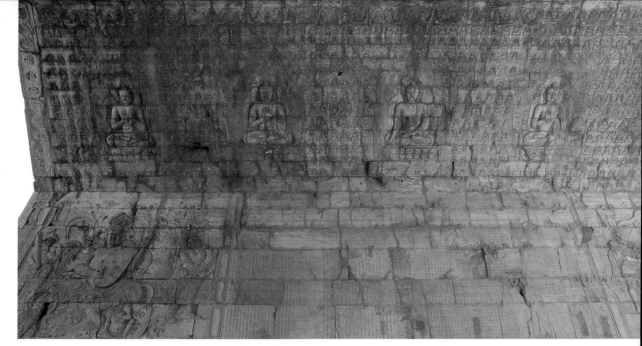

**石刻浮雕** 云台券洞内雕刻着四大天王、十方佛、千佛等佛像,其间刻有梵、藏、八思巴、维吾尔、西夏和汉六种文字题刻的《陀罗尼经咒》、《造塔功德记》等石刻,是现存稀有而精美的元代艺术杰作。

**Stone carvings** Carved in relief on the stone wall of the arched passage of the Cloud Terrace are images of the Four Heavenly Kings, Buddhas of Ten Directions and 1,000 Buddhas. There are also inscribed Buddhist scriptures in Sanskrit, Tibetan, Basiba, Uygur, Xixia and Chinese languages.

长城夕照

Great Wall at sunset.

**八达岭长城** 是明万里长城具有代表性的精华地段。平均高度为 7.8 米，墙基厚约 6.5 米，墙顶平均宽约 5.8 米，气势雄伟，是中国最早开发旅游的长城地段之一。

**Great Wall at Badaling** This is the best preserved part of the Great Wall. It is 7.8 meters high, 6.5 meters thick and 5.8 meters wide on the top. Badaling is the first section of the Great Wall opened to tourists.

**春到长城**　春日塞垣南北,山堆青黛、桃李争艳,成了锦绣之乡。

**Great Wall in spring**　The mountains along the Great Wall are decorated with peach and plum blossoms.

**八达岭之秋** 层林尽染，五彩缤纷，巨龙唱欢歌。

**Great Wall in autumn** In the fall tree leaves turn into various colors.

**雪雕**　冬令飞雪,山岭间长垣如白龙飞腾,寒光
照射,分外妖娆。

**Great Wall in winter**　The Great Wall covered in
snow looks like a silver dragon undulating on
mountain ridges.

放飞

Flying kite on the Great Wall

**城墙** 八达岭南段城墙大都用整齐巨大条石和大城砖砌筑,内充泥土石块夯实。据城墙残存石刻记载,当时是调用军工分段包修,用几千名官兵和许多农夫,半年左右才修筑 70 多丈,可见工程之艰巨。

**A section of the Great Wall** The part of the Great Wall at Badaling is lined with huge stone slabs and filled with rammed earth and rocks. An inscription on a stone tablet unearthed at Badaling records that several thousand soldiers and peasants built only 23 meters of the Great Wall in six months.

**璀璨飞龙** 图中长城有如神龙夜游,极富魅力, 是深得中外游客赞赏的又一景观。

**Great Wall at night** Now electric lights have been strung' along the Great Wall at Badaling, presenting a splendid scene at night.

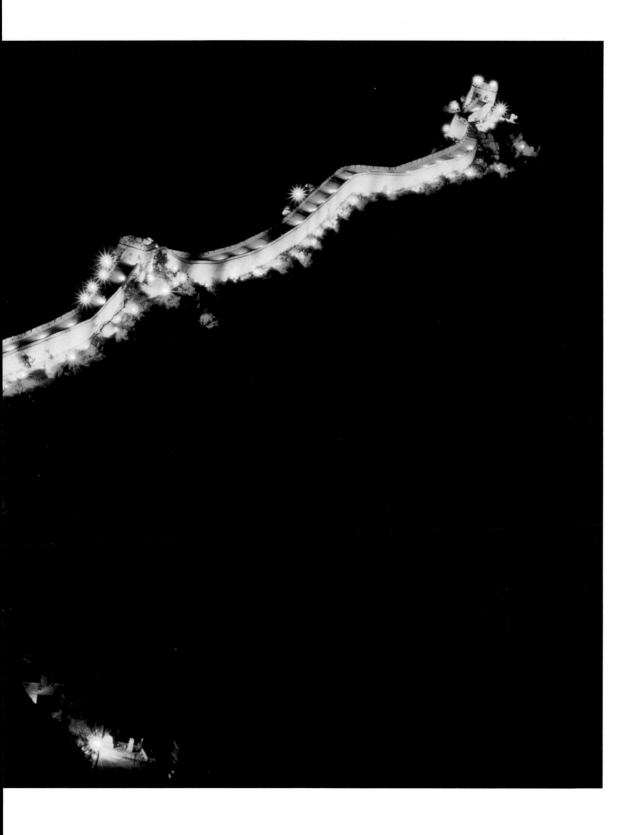

**梯道**　在山势陡峭的地方,城墙顶上筑成梯形,称作"梯道"。八达岭长城上的梯道,从两山直泻峡谷,势如游龙啸天,巨蟒窜洞,长达千米,蔚为壮观。

**'Ladder Path'**　A part of the Great Wall at Badaling runs on a steep mountain ridge. Its top rises step by step like a ladder. It falls directly down to the deep gullies over 1,000 meters.

**垛口**　长城靠内部的一面,用砖砌成高约 1 米的宇墙(或叫女墙)。靠外的一面则用砖砌成高近 2 米的垛口。每个垛口上部有一个口,叫瞭望口;下部有个小洞,叫射洞,是用来射击敌人的。

**Battlements**　Parapets stand on the inner side of the Great Wall and on the outer side are battlements of two meters high. Under the crenels are apertures for archers.

**危崖耸峙** 长城营造者在陡立而不规则的山崖上砌就了一座敌台，扼险防守。

**Watch Bay** Such defense works on the Great Wall were built on sheer and irregular mountain projections of strategic importance.

**敌楼**　敌楼是指筑于长城城墙内侧，可以屯住戍边士卒的建筑物。

**Watch tower**　Watch towers are located at regular intervals on the Great Wall. The defense soldiers lived in them.

**敌楼内景**　图为空心敌楼内景,楼内正中有一木顶小室,四面是砖砌小拱券,尽头是箭窗。

**Inside a watch tower**　This is one kind of the watch towers on the Great Wall. In the middle of it is a small house with a wooden roof. All around there are holes for shooting arrows.

**铁炮**　八达岭长城入口处旁,有几门明代制造的铁炮。图为其一。

**Iron cannons**　Several iron cannons made during the Ming Dynasty are placed at the entrance to Badaling Pass.

# 慕田峪长城

　　慕田峪长城位于北京怀柔县西北,距市区 70 公里,西接居庸关,东连古北口,是万里长城又一精华所在。明洪武元年(公元 1368 年),徐达奉命筑长城,自山海关抵慕田峪。永乐二年(公元 1404 年)建关。嘉靖三十年(公元 1551 年),加设昌镇,东起慕田峪。这样,慕田峪长城成了蓟镇和昌镇长城的交接处,其位置重要可见。

　　慕田峪长城的特点是双边垛口,还建有"支城"。所谓"支城",就是在长城内外侧山梁高脊处,再节外生枝顺势修出一段长城,或几米,或几十米,并筑有敌楼,当地人称为"刀把楼"。两侧都有垛口,可同时设置滚木礌石,攻守自如;修筑"刀把楼",可控制制高点,缓解对主城的威胁。

　　慕田峪长城的另一个特点是林木葱郁、水草丰茂,风景异常优美。在人们的印象中,似乎所有的长城都在荒山野岭之上,殊不知慕田峪长城却躺在万绿丛中。这里一年四季都有美景可供欣赏。春天是群芳争艳,桃红李白;夏天是漫山青绿、郁郁葱葱;冬天是白雪皑皑,松柏傲霜;而最迷人的则是金色的秋天,核桃、板栗、梨子等果实累累,挂满枝头,加上各种树木的叶子有金黄、鲜红、绛紫,五彩缤纷,漫山弥谷,富有高山园林的意趣。

# The Great Wall at Mutianyu

This section of the Great Wall lies to the northwest of the county seat of Huairou, 70 kilometers from downtown Beijing. To its west is Juyongguan Pass and to its east is Gubeikou. General Xu Da of the Ming Dynasty began the construction of the Great Wall from Shanhaiguan to Mutianyu in 1368 and built Mutianyu Pass in 1404. Changzhen Garrison was set up in 1551. The section of the Great Wall at Mutianyu became a strategic point at the juncture of Jizhen Garrison and Changzhen Garrison.

Two unique features of this section are the "double battlements" and "branch walls". On top of the wall on both sides there are battlements with crenels. At some places where the mountain ridge branches out there are protrusions of the Great Wall for several meters or several dozen meters long on which there are watch towers. The watch towers on the "branch walls" controlled high vantage points to protect the main part of the Great Wall.

The Mutianyu area has dense woods and rich pastures. The landscape is beautiful all year round. In spring peach and plum blossoms decorate the mountain sides; in summer visitors feel cool amidst the luxuriant green of trees and grass; in autumn, fruits—walnuts, chestnuts and pears—are ripe and the tree leaves are of various colors— golden, red and crimson; and in winter snow presents another attractive scene over the Great Wall.

**慕田峪长城** 此段长城极其壮观。墙体为条石砌筑，垛口为青砖垒砌，十分坚固。一般长城为外侧垛口，内侧女墙；慕田峪长城则全部是双面垛口，为其他地方所罕见。

**Great Wall at Mutianyu** The wall is of stone slabs and the top has grey brick battlements. Other parts of the Great Wall has battlements only on the outer side and parapets on the inner side. But this section has battlements on both sides.

慕田峪关　即正关台,关口处三座空心敌楼通连并矗,两侧楼体的楼室窄小, 正中楼室宽大, 体高势伟。楼上建有望亭, 构造雄奇新颖, 颇为罕见。

**Mutianyu Pass**　Three watch towers stand at the entrance to the pass one next to another. The middle tower is very spacious inside. On its top is a pavilion.

古城晨雾　　　Ancient town in early morning.

**正关台内景**　全部为砖石结构,墙壁设箭窗瞭望口,易守难攻。

**Inside Mutianyu Pass**　The castle is built with stone slabs and bricks. There are apertures in the wall for archers.

**巍巍雪城**　雪盖长城,更显长城雄姿。　**Great Wall covered in snow.**

**秋到慕田峪** 秋日,层林尽染,古城生辉。

**Mutianyu in autumn** Colorful tree leaves enhance the beauty of the Great Wall.

**牛犄角边** 在关城西北侧,山势险峭,长城从东山下来,向西从山腰奔向近千米的山顶,后又翻身回转朝下返向山腰,因形似牛角,人称"牛犄角边"。

**'Horn Corner'** It is a loop of the Great Wall to the northwest of Mutianyu Pass. The Great Wall comes down from a mountain to the east and goes up to another mountain top for nearly 1,000 meters, and then goes down again to make a turn like a bull horn.

牛犄角边日出

Sunrise at 'Horn Corner'.

**鹰飞倒仰** 是慕田峪长城一绝。这段长城在
"牛犄角边"西侧,城体全建在岩石裸露的悬崖
峭壁上,远望似一只仰身上飞的雄鹰,故名。

**'Eagle Flying Up Side Down'** A short part of the
Great Wall perches on a sheer cliff of bare rock
and from a distance looks like an eagle flying upside down.

**修复长城** 长城历经千百年的风风雨雨,很多地段已残破不堪,图为 1985 年修复慕田峪长城的情景,人们正扒掉残破的墙体,以便码砌新砖。

**Great Wall under repair** Many parts of the Great Wall have collapsed through the years. Large funds have been spent on its restoration. The picture shows a repair at Mutianyu in 1985.

长城变奏曲

Great Wall seen from another angle.

**城砖**　是明代才普遍使用的一种建筑材料，以粘土烧制。修长城所用砖有的重达几十斤，主要用于包砌墙身、铺墙面和修建敌楼。

**Bricks from the Great Wall**　The bricks of this kind were used during the Ming Dynasty. A piece may be as heavy as several dozen kilograms. They were used to line the wall and build watch tower.

**长城石雷**　石雷是把石头的中间掏空，里边装上火药制成的，用于守城。敌兵一旦攻到长城下，守城士兵就将石雷引信点着，扔到城下，石雷一炸，石片横飞，杀伤力很大。

**Stone mines**　When invading troops were at the foot of the Great Wall, the defenders would detonate stone mines and throw them down. Gunpowder inside would explode.

雪里将军

'Army general' in snow.

涧口长城　　Great Wall at Jiankou.

涧口长城雪景　Great Wall at Jiankou in winter.

云梯

A 'ladder' on the Great Wall.

刀把楼

A watch tower on a 'branch wall'.

缥缈

**Great Wall shrouded in mist**

**黄花镇**　位于北京怀柔县西北，距北京城区 60 公里，境内有长城 10.8 公里，是明代南卫京师、西卫皇陵的"极为紧要之区"。

**Huanghua Town**　The town lies to the county seat of Huairou, 60 kilometers from downtown Beijing. A section of the Great Wall runs inside the town for 10.8 kilometers. It was a vital place in defending Beijing and the imperial cemetery during the Ming Dynasty.

**黄花城长城**  城体无现代一砖一石,构筑雄险,历史沧桑感完整,是一独具特色的长城旅游点。

**Great Wall in Huanghua Town**  This section has retained all its original bricks and stone slabs without any modern building materials. It has become a much loved tourist spot.

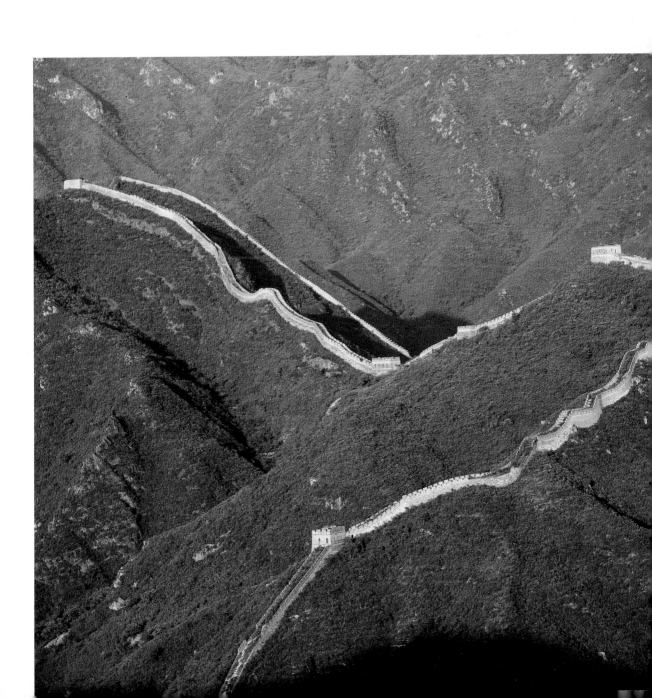

**雉堞** 城墙垛口鳞次栉比,富于韵律美。

**Crenels** The battlements on the Great Wall rise and fall at a rhythm.

相映成趣

**An harmonious pair.**

黄花城西边西水峪景象　　　Xishui Valley to the west of Huanghua Town.

**九孔楼**　位于北京怀柔县与延庆县交界处,是明长城建筑规模和形制最大的一座敌楼。为方形上下两层空心结构,条石基座上的楼体系青砖砌筑。楼四面墙壁都有箭窗,每面并排 9 个,共 36 个。惜今已圮坍。

**Nine-Hole Tower**　Located on the boundary between Huairou and Yanqing counties, the largest watch tower on the Great Wall built during the Ming Dynasty once stood on a base of stone slabs. It was built with grey bricks. On each of the four walls there were nine holes for archers.

# 金山岭长城

　　金山岭长城横亘在北京密云县与河北省滦平县交界地带,距北京133公里。据说因此段长城上建有大、小金山楼而得名。传说修建这两座敌楼的是当年随戚继光(公元 1528～1587 年)北上的三千名江浙军士,因思念家乡,故借用镇江大、小金山岛的名字命名这两座敌楼,以寄托对故土的眷恋之情。

　　金山岭长城全长 13 公里,有敌楼 90 余座,一般 100 米左右一座,在地形复杂处,有的甚至仅间距 50～60 米,其密集程度为其他地段所罕见。

　　严密的防御体系是金山岭长城的一大特点。长城的修建者在城墙以北的制高点上设置烽火台,并把长城外侧的山坡铲削,用石块砌筑重城(也叫拦马墙),城上设关口和空心敌楼,组成了城关相联、敌台相望、重城防卫、烽火报警的防御体系。金山岭长城地势险要,设防严谨,建造艺术精美,故称"第二八达岭"。

# The Great Wall at Jinshanling

　　The section of the Great Wall at Jinshanling stretches from Miyun County of Beijing to Luanping County of Hebei Province, 133 kilometers from downtown Beijing. The name came from two towers—Greater Jinshan and Lesser Jinshan—on the Great Wall in this region. Three thousand soldiers under General Qi Jiguang (1528-1587), all natives of Jiangsu and Zhejiang provinces, built the two watch towers and named them after Greater Jinshan Island and Lesser Jinshan Island in their homeland.

　　The section of the Great Wall at Jinshanling is 13 kilometers long with 90 watch towers at an interval of 100 meters. At some places with more complex terrain the interval is only 50 to 60 meters. Such a density is rare on the entire length of the Great Wall.

　　The terrain in the Jinshanling area is complex. Its defense was especially strong. On every vantage point north of the Great Wall many beacon towers were built. The immediate area before the Great Wall was leveled to build a shorter wall with stone slabs. The defense was thus further enhanced.

**古北口**　位于北京密云县北部,是通向内蒙及东北的重要关口,它背依盘龙、卧虎二山,万里长城主体城墙将二山连成一线,形势奇险。

**Gubeikou Pass**　The pass north of the county seat of Huairou used to be a vital point on the road from Inner Mongolia and Northeast China to Beijing. It straddles Panlong and Wohu Mountains to form a strategic outpost.

萧萧古城墙

**Ancient city wall.**

**圆敌台**　古北口长城
残存的圆敌台，为其
他地方所罕见。

**A round watch bay**
Such defense works are
found only in the
Gubeikou area along
the Great Wall.

**金山岭长城** 位于古北口以东约 7.5 公里处,长城似巨龙环卧于群山之巅,它那腾挪跌宕、绵延逶迤的磅礴气势,令人振奋。

**Great Wall at Jinshanling** The Great Wall at Jinshanling runs through mountain peaks for 7.5 kilometers from Gubeikou Pass.

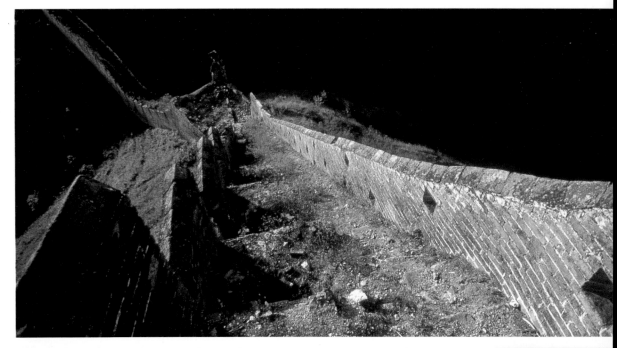

雪后长城　　Great Wall after a snowfall.

**鹤立**　未修复的金山岭长城上,一座残破的敌楼仅剩下不规则的一角,恰似一只仙鹤在此小憩。

**A lonely watch tower**　The ruins of a watch tower look like a crane taking a short rest here.

**长城金辉**　旭日凭临长城而出,彩霞初照,呈现出古老沉静神秘莫测的意境。

**A brilliant Great Wall**　The early morning sunlight gives the place a feeling of mystery.

**三眼楼** 空心敌楼分上、下两层,第一层用来住宿和存放兵器,大都设有数目不等的箭窗,敌楼的名称往往由箭窗多少来定,如图中敌楼一面有三个箭窗,故名三眼楼。上层墙面有垛口、瞭望孔和射洞,用来守望和射击。

**Three-Hole Tower**　A watch tower is usually of two stories. The ground floor was used to store weapons and had a number of windows for archers. The upper floor has peep-holes and apertures for archers. This watch tower has three arrow holes in the wall of the ground floor.

长城中秋月

**Great Wall under a bright autumn moon.**

**海市蜃楼** 古城墙、敌楼在云海中若隐若现,疑入蓬莱仙境。

**Great Wall in clouds** The ancient wall and watch towers shrouded in mist and clouds look like a scene of mirage.

**金兽吠天**　多数空心敌楼上层中间有一座小房子，叫铺房，供守城士兵遮风避雨。其房顶采用仿木结构，垂脊上亦有一溜垂脊兽，它们昂首向天，气势非凡。

**Roof ridge decorations**　Most of the watch towers have a small house on the top to shelter defending soldiers. Its roof ridges are decorated with animal sculptures.

**库房楼**　是金山岭长城最有代表性的一座敌楼。设有战台、挡马墙和火炮防御墙等三道防线，坚固异常。

**Storage Tower**　This is a representative kind of watch towers on the Great Wall at Jinshanling with battlements, "blocking the horse wall" and iron cannons.

**障墙** 即在垛口墙内侧加设的一排排垂直于垛口的短墙，墙高2.5米左右，墙上有瞭望口和射孔。当敌人攻上城墙时，守城士兵可据守障墙，步步为营进行抵抗。

**Barrier wall** A wall of 2.5 meters high runs on the top of the Great Wall parallel to the battlements. It has peep-holes and arrow holes and served as the second barrier when the enemy had climbed up the Great Wall.

敌楼内景

Inside a watch tower.

**相依** 图中残破敌楼转角处,似一对夫妇相依相偎,情真意切。

**Remains of a watch tower** The corner of the collapsed watch tower looks like a husband and wife embracing.

# 司马台长城

　　司马台长城位于北京密云县北 77 公里处的东庄禾乡境内,距北京 120 公里,东起望京楼,西与金山岭长城相连,全长 19 公里,有敌楼 35 座,雄伟壮观。

　　司马台长城构思精巧,设计奇特,具有军事、建筑、艺术等多方面科学考察价值,它集万里长城特色于一地,形成一段"奇妙的长城"。此段长城多建于刀劈斧削般的峰巅危崖之上。有的攀伏于几乎达九十度的陡峭岩脊上,登长城犹如上"天梯"、过"天桥",险而又险。1986 年在密云县举行的长城论证会上,中国长城专家罗哲文说:"司马台长城是长城之最"。

# The Great Wall at Simatai

　　The section of the Great Wall at Simatai lies in Dongzhuanghe Township, 77 kilometers to the north of the county seat of Miyun and 120 kilometers from downtown Beijing. It begins at Watching the Capital Tower in the east and joins the Great Wall at Jinshanling in the west over 19 kilometers. The 35 watch towers on this section are very magnificent.

　　The design of this section is ingenious, valuable for the study of military affairs, construction and art of the time. Great part of the Great Wall here is on sheer cliffs, some of which rise at an angle of 90 degrees. Luo Zhewen, a Chinese expert on the Great Wall, commented at a symposium on the Great Wall held in Miyun County in 1986: "The Great Wall at Simatai is the greatest of the whole length."

司马台长城　　Great Wall at Simatai.

**山水长城**　司马台水库位于司马台关门外,自然把长城分为东西两段,使长城如二龙戏水,更添新姿。

**Simatai Reservoir**　The reservoir outside the gate of Simatai Pass divides the Great Wall into two parts.

**大地走红艺术**　中国大地艺术在长城上。

**Red Earth Art**　An artistic show on the Great Wall.

单边　因长城所经山脊高耸且十分狭窄，前后坡极陡，所以只在悬崖外侧修了一道薄墙，称为单边。墙上置有上、中、下三排射孔及礌石孔，并增筑了障墙，加强了防御功能。

'Single-Sided Wall'　Some places are so narrow on the mountain ridges only a thin wall could be built on the outer side of a cliff. Such a wall has three layers of holes for archers and a barrier wall.

天桥　在山顶悬崖绝壁处，长 100 米，宽仅 0.3 米，两侧是悬崖绝壁，险绝异常。

'Heavenly Bridge'　This bridge over a precipice is 100 meters long and only 0.3 meters wide.

好汉过天桥

**Brave people over 'Heavenly Bridge'**

**望京楼** 是司马台长城的制高点,它屹立在海拔近千米的山巅上。晴晚眺望,可见北京城的灯火,故名。

**Watching the Capital Tower** It is located on a vantage point nearly 1,000 meters above sea level. In a clear night one can see the lights in Beijing from the tower.

**天梯**　是单面墙体,长约 50 米,坡陡,墙窄,呈直梯状沿山脊上升,直通云天,当地人称为天梯。

**'Heavenly Ladder'**　This thin section of the Great Wall is 50 meters long and rises up a sharp climb. Local people call it 'Heavenly Ladder'.

**单边韵律**　司马台长城共有三段单边墙,此段位于望京楼和仙女楼之间,长约 300 米,砌在形如刀刃的山脊上,尤为险要。

**'Single-Sided Wall'**　There are three such "Single-Sided Walls" in the Simatai area. This one is found between Watching the Capital Tower and Fairy Maid Tower. It is about 300 meters long on top of a precipitous cliff.

**敌楼**　图中敌楼设计巧妙,两侧皆无门与城墙相通。欲进此楼,必须由城墙内侧砖券拱门而出,沿岩石小径至楼下,然后登攀临时设置的小梯,方可爬入比箭窗大不了多少的楼门里。这样,增强了敌楼的防御功能。

**A watch tower**　This cleverly designed watch tower has no doors on either side to the top of the Great Wall. It can be entered only through a tunnel in the wall along a tiny path and a narrow ladder. The entrance is no wider than a hole for archers.

**仙女楼**　位于望京楼西,是敌楼中建造得最美的一座,因传说一只美丽的羚羊变成仙女住在此楼,与放羊倌相恋,故名。

**Fairy Maid Tower**　Located to the west of Watching the Capital Tower, it is the most graceful watch tower on the Great Wall. A folk tale says an antelope and a fairy maid once lived in it. The fairy maid fell in love with a local shepherd.

小鸟欢唱

**Chirping birds.**

**铭文砖**　司马台长城上有数以万计的文字青砖,上面刻有"万历伍年石塘路造"、"万历七年德州营造"等字样,其数量之多,为其他地区所少见。这些文字砖,是今人了解明长城建造的珍贵文物,具有很高的价值。

**Brick inscription**　There are more than 10,000 bricks on the Great Wall at Simatai that bear inscriptions noting the date and maker of the bricks. Such a large number of inscribed bricks is rarely seen in other parts of the Great Wall.

# 山海关和嘉峪关

山海关，即举世闻名的"天下第一关"，位于河北省秦皇岛市东北15公里，为华北通往东北的咽喉所在。古人有诗赞曰："两京锁钥无双地，万里长城第一关。"

习惯上，将山海关视为万里长城的东部起点，事实并非如此。究其原因，一是明洪武十四年(公元1381年)徐达修筑长城时首先把东端起点确定在这里，辽东镇长城是正统(公元1436～1449年)初年才开始修筑的。再是清朝时，修筑较简单的辽东长城大多圮塌，而由山海关往西的长城却依然坚固，保存较好，又有雄伟的山海关和嘉峪关东西对峙，所以才形成了山海关是长城最东端的习惯说法。

嘉峪关在甘肃省的西部，是明代万里长城的西端终点。明洪武五年(公元1372年)宋国公征西大将军冯胜率兵进军河西，他沿途巡视，最后看中了嘉峪关依山傍水，四面地域开阔，宜于建关的险要地形，奏朝廷弃敦煌不守，而筑嘉峪关城。这样，嘉峪关一线的战略地位便比任何时候都重要了。经过明代数百年的经营，嘉峪关以"天下雄关"的威名而声扬四海。它是现存长城全线中规模最宏伟、保存最完整的关城。

# Shanhaiguan Pass and Jiayuguan Pass

Shanhaiguan Pass, known as "the First Pass Under Heaven", is situated 15 kilometers to the northeast of Qinhuangdao City in Hebei Province. Its strategic importance in ancient times is described in a poem: "It is the key to the capital and the first pass of the Great Wall."

Shanhaiguan Pass is commonly taken as the eastern end of the Great Wall. The reason is that when General Xu Da of the Ming Dynasty rebuilt the Great Wall in 1381 he set the eastern end of it at Shanhaiguan. The section of Liaodong Garrison was built later between 1439 and 1449. Another reason is that the section of the Great Wall in Liaodong Peninsula had already collapsed during the Qing Dynasty. But the Great Wall west of Shanhaiguan had remained intact. As a result most people think the eastern end of the Great Wall is at Shanhaiguan.

Jiayuguan Pass in western Gansu Province was the western end of the Great Wall during the Ming Dynasty. When General Feng Sheng, Duke of Song of the Ming Dynasty was on an inspection tour in 1372 he chose Jiayuguan as the site for a pass for the area was broad and flat. The pass was reinforced constantly through the nearly 300 years of the rule of the Ming Dynasty and called "the Strategic Pass Under Heaven". It is now the best preserved and largest pass of the Great Wall.

**天下第一关** 即山海关东门,门上建有高两层的箭楼,其正额为"天下第一关"五个大字,系明成化八年(公元1472年)进士萧显所书,字迹苍劲雄浑,极能表现这一带的巍巍气势。

**'The First Pass Under Heaven'**  The eastern gate of Shanhaiguan Pass has a two-story tower. A plaque over the entrance of the tower is inscribed with five Chinese characters meaning "the First Pass Under Heaven". They are in the handwriting of Xiao Xian, a successful imperial examination candidate.

**山海关城**　平面呈四方形,城墙外部以青砖包砌,内填夯土,高约 14 米, 宽 7 米, 有城门四个。它襟山带海, 雄姿凛凛, 气势磅礴, 堪称天下第一。

**Shanhaiguan Pass**　The square castle wall is lined with grey bricks and filled with rammed earth. It is 14 meters high and seven meters wide. Four gates are located in the middle of the four sides.

**瓮城** 指在城门外侧加筑的凸出于城墙外的小城圈。它是关城的防御堡垒,用来驻军和存放武器。山海关四座城门外均有瓮城,现仅存东门瓮城。

**Citadel** It is a small enclosure guarding the entrance of Shanhaiguan Pass. It had living quarters for soldiers and storages for weapons and army supplies.

**老龙头长城** 系中国名将戚继光为防海盗而从山海关延筑过来的入海边墙,建于明嘉靖年间(公元 1522~1566 年)。长城在这里陡入海口,形势非常险要。

**'Old Dragon Head'** This section of the Great Wall was built between 1522 and 1566 by famous army commander Qi Jiguang to ward off pirates.

**护城河** 山海关城外有宽约 17 米、深 8 米有余的护城河围绕,坚上加坚,固上加固,形成一个层层加防的防御体系。

**Moat** The moat around Shanhaiguan pass is 17 meters wide and eight meters deep as an additional defense barrier of the pass.

**瑞莲捧日**　山海关名景之一。每当破晓,太阳初跃海面,红云四拥,景致十分壮美。

**'Lotus Flower and Sun'**　At dawn the sea bathes in crimson glow of the sunshine at this spot. It has become a famous tourist attraction at Shanhaiguan.

**九门口** 位于山海关城东北 15 公里处,是明蓟镇长城的重要关隘,因有一座九个水门的过河 城桥而得名。它与山海关唇齿相依,历史上曾 是东北进入中原的咽喉。

**Jiumen Pass** Located 15 kilometers to the northeast of Shanghaiguan Pass, it used to have nine water entrances. Its location on the road between Northeast to North China was once as important as Shanhaiguan Pass during the Ming Dynasty.

**澄海楼**　位于宁海城上,是登临观海的绝佳处。清康熙(公元 1661～1722 年在位)、乾隆(公元 1735～1795 年在位)等皇帝曾多次登临澄海楼饮酒赋诗,此楼因此名扬天下。

**Chenghai Tower**　The tower on top of the city wall of Ninghai is a good place to watch the sea. Emperors Kang Xi（1661-1722）and Qian Long（1735-1795）came to this tower several times, raising its fame.

**宁海城** 位于老龙头北,为戚继光所修扼海关城。原城已毁,图为修复后的宁海城。

**Ninghai City** It was built by General Qi Jiguang to control the seashore to the north of Old Dragon Head. The city has been restored.

**孟姜女坟** 山海关东南入海0.5公里处，有礁石冒出水面，人们附称为"姜女坟"。孟姜女是中国民间传说中的贞女烈妇，传说其夫在此修筑长城，劳累致死，孟姜女恸不欲生，哭倒长城后投海自尽。

**Tomb of Meng Jiangnu** Two rocks, one higher than the other, rise above the sea 0.5 kilometers from the shore near Shanhaiguan Pass and are called by the locals Tomb of Meng Jiangnu. She came to the construction site of the Great Wall to mourn over her husband who died of hard labor building the Great Wall. She cried so hard a section of the Great Wall collapsed. She then drowned herself in the sea.

**孟姜女塑像** 供奉于孟姜女庙前殿。庙位于山海关城东6.5公里处的望夫石村，用以祭祀孟姜女。庙分前、后两殿，规模不大而小巧玲珑。图中孟姜女塑像供于前殿。

**Statue of Meng Jiangnu** The Temple of Meng Jiangnu is located in Wangfushi Village, 6.5 kilometers east of Shanhaiguan Pass. The statue is in the front hall of the two halls of the temple.

**望夫石** 位于孟姜女庙后殿前,传说是孟姜女登临望夫的地方,石上有传说中孟姜女的"脚印"和"泪痕",并刻着清乾隆皇帝所题七律诗一首。

**Longing for Husband Stone** A local tale says Meng Jiangnu, wife of a construction worker of the Great Wall who died of hard labor, stood here to wait for here husband to return to life.

**角山长城** 角山位于山海关北门外 3 公里处,是明代万里长城翻越的第一座山峦,因而被称为万里长城第一山。角山长城随山势起伏,宛如一条游龙,飞舞在山中。

**Great Wall at Jiaoshan** This section of the Great Wall three kilometers outside the northern gate of Shanhaiguan Pass goes into the first mountain on its westward travel.

**长城倒挂** 又称三道关，位于山海关北约 4 公里处，长城如游龙巨蟒从角山逶迤而下，直插谷底，又随即依山傍崖蜿蜒而上，似倒挂在半空中，是长城风光一绝。

**'Great Wall Upside Down'** The spot is found four kilometers north of Shanhaiguan Pass where the Great Wall climbs down to a deep valley as if it hung down the mountain side.

**烽火台** 古代边防上,供燃点烽火用以报警的高台。台上有一种木制机具叫桔槔,可以升到高处。桔槔上配着一种笼子叫兜零,里边装上些草、硫磺、狼粪等物,遇有敌情,白天燃烟,夜间点火,通报邻近的烽火台。

**A beacon tower** A wooden pulley could lift a basket filled with dry grass, wolf droppings and sulphur to the top of the tower. When enemy troops were approaching the defending soldiers would send fire signals by relay of beacon towers to their commanders.

**长城入海处** 位于山海关南4公里处,它孤兀海中,波摇涛撼,历来被视为区域风光一绝。

**Where the Great Wall enters the sea** The actual eastern end of the Great Wall is in the sea, four kilometers to the south of Shanhaiguan Pass.

**嘉峪关全景** 关城由内城、瓮城、罗城和外城组成。内城居关城正中，平面为梯形，西头大、东头小。有东、西二门，上建城楼。四隅有角台，上建砖砌角楼。远远望去，整座关城巍楼高峙，台堡林立，极为壮观。

**Jiayuguan Pass** The pass is made up with an inner city, a citadel and an outer city. The inner city in the middle of the pass has a trapezoidal layout tapering to the east and two gates with gate towers and a watch tower on each of the four corners.

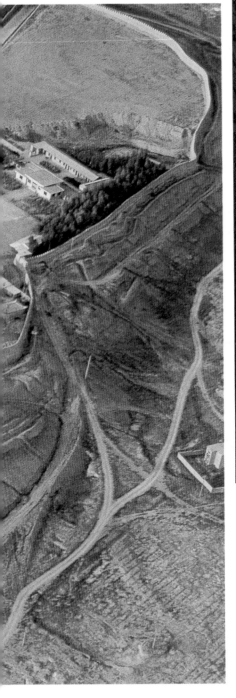

**城楼** 面宽三间,周围设廊,高约 17 米,为三层单檐歇山顶式建筑。楼顶翘出的四角戗脊上安设着栩栩如生的吻兽,为关城平添了装饰色彩。

**A city gate tower** The three-story tower is 17 meters high with a gabled roof and surrounded by a corridor. Animal sculptures decorate the four roof ridges.

**嘉峪关夯土长城**　嘉峪关附近长城大部土筑，高约六米许。现多已残破。

**Great Wall of rammed earth at Jiayuguan**　Most part of the Great Wall near Jiayuguan is of rammed earth. The collapsed wall used to be six meters high.

嘉峪关日出　　**Sunrise over Jiayuguan Pass**

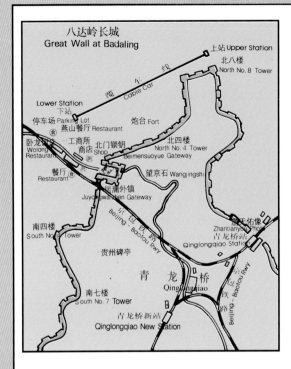

**八达岭长城**
**Great Wall at Badaling**

上站 Upper Station

北八楼
North No. 8 Tower

缆车线 Cable Car

Lower Station
下站

停车场 Parking Lot

燕山餐厅 Restaurant

炮台 Fort

卧龙松
Wolong
Restaurant

工商所
商店
Shop

北门锁钥
Beimensuoyue Gateway

北四楼
North No. 4 Tower

餐厅
Restaurant

望京石 Wangjingshi

居庸外镇
Juyongwaizhen Gateway

詹天佑像
Zhantianyou Photo

青龙桥站
Qinglongqiao Station

南四楼
South No. 4 Tower

北京—包头铁路
Beijing - Baotou Rwy

京张铁路
Beijing - Baotou Rwy

贵州碑亭

青龙桥
Qinglongqiao

南七楼
South No. 7 Tower

青龙桥新站
Qinglongqiao New Station

**慕田峪长城**
**Great Wall at Mutianyu**

烽火台
Beacon Tower

莲花池
Lianhua Pool

珍珠泉 Zhenzhu Spring

龙潭 Longtan Pool

缆车线 Cable Car

慕城步道

正关台 Zhengguan Tower

Restaurant 外宾餐厅
Yanjing Painting Studio 燕京书画社
Restaurant 内宾餐厅
Parking Lot No.1 第一停车场
售票处
Booking office
第二停车场
Park NO.2

售票处
Booking office

鸳鸯松
Yuanyang Pine

迎宾松
Yingbin Pine

慕田峪
旅游服务处

慕田峪村

石臼
Shijiu

**金山岭长城位置图**
**Great Wall at Jinshanling**

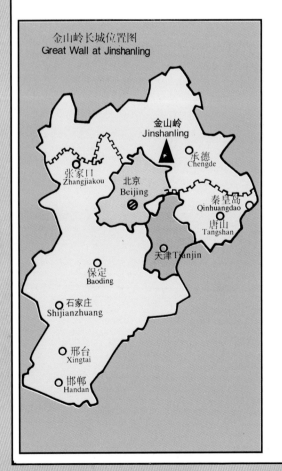

金山岭
Jinshanling

承德
Chengde

张家口
Zhangjiakou

北京
Beijing

秦皇岛
Qinhuangdao

唐山
Tangshan

天津 Tianjin

保定
Baoding

石家庄
Shijianzhuang

邢台
Xingtai

邯郸
Handan

**居庸关（云台）**
**Juyongguan（Yuntai）Great Wall**

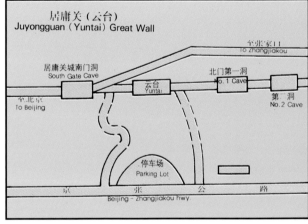

至张家口
To Zhangjiakou

居庸关城南门洞
South Gate Cave

云台
Yuntai

北门第一洞
No. 1 Cave

第二洞
No. 2 Cave

至北京
To Beijing

停车场
Parking Lot

京　　张　　公　　路
Beijing - Zhangjiakou hwy

**司马台长城**
**Simatai Great Wall**

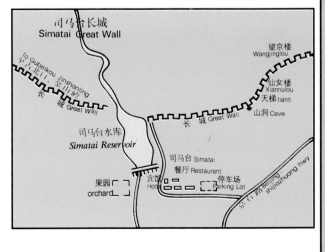

望京楼
Wangjinglou

仙女楼
Xiannulou

天梯 tianti

山洞 Cave

To Gubeikou Jinshanling
至古北口金山岭

长城 Great Wall

长城 Great Wall

司马台水库
*Simatai Reservoir*

司马台 Simatai
餐厅 Restaurant

宾馆
Hotel

停车场
Parking Lot

京承路 Beijing
shijiazhuang hwy

果园
orchard

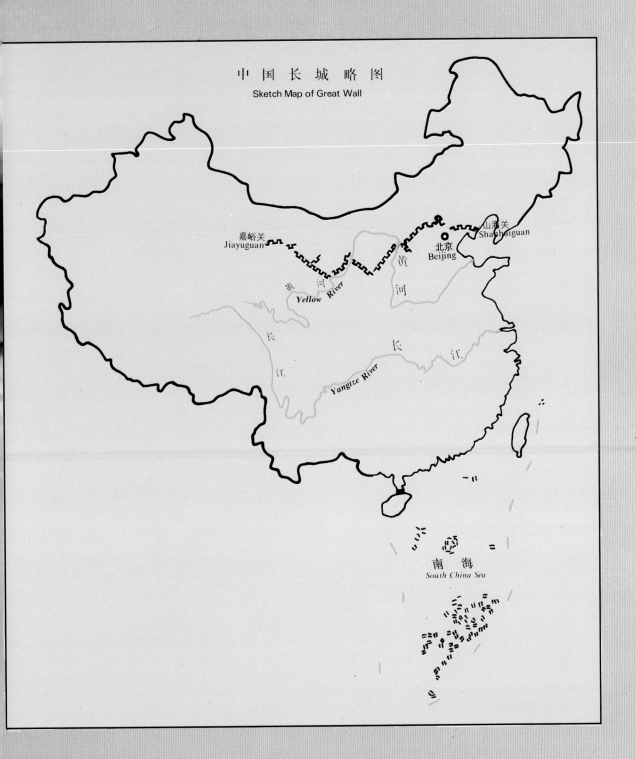

中 国 长 城 略 图
Sketch Map of Great Wall

嘉峪关
Jiayuguan

山海关
Shanhaiguan

北京
Beijing

黄河
黄 河

黄 河
Yellow River

长江

长 江
长 江
Yangtze River

南 海
South China Sea

编　　辑　施永南
**责任编辑**　望天星
**翻　　译**　刘宗仁
**摄　　影**　严欣强　罗文发
　　　　　　翟东风　周幼马
　　　　　　刘世昭　万　戈
　　　　　　李　芬　胡维标
　　　　　　姜景余　高明义
　　　　　　张肇基　王春树
　　　　　　何炳富　高光宇
　　　　　　董宗贵
**装帧设计**　望天星


**Editor:** Shi Yongnan
**Editor in Charge:** Wang Tianxing
**Translated by:** Liu Zongren
**Photos by:** Yan Xinqiang, Luo Wenfa,
　　　　　　Zhai Dongfeng, Zhou Youma,
　　　　　　Liu Shizhao, Wan Ge,
　　　　　　Li Fen, Hu Weibiao,
　　　　　　Jiang Jingyu, Gao Mingyi,
　　　　　　Zhang Zhaoji, Wang Chunshu,
　　　　　　He Bingfu, Gao Guangyu
　　　　　　and Dong Zonggui
**Designed by:** Wang Tianxing

**图书在版编目(CIP)数据**

北京长城:中、英对照/施永南编;刘宗仁译.
北京:中国世界语出版社,1996.11
ISBN 7 - 5052 - 0316 - 9

I. 北…　II.①施…②刘…
III. 长城－摄影集－汉、英 IV.K928.71－64

中国版本图书馆 CIP 数据核字(96)第 18639 号


**北京长城**

中国世界语出版社出版

北京百花印刷厂印制

中国国际图书贸易总公司(国际书店)发行

(中国北京车公庄西路 35 号)

邮政信箱第 399 号 邮政编码 100044

ISBN 7 - 5052 - 0316 - 9/K.53

05000
**85 - CE - 500P**